D1162648

WITHDRAWN
FROM THE RECORDS OF THE
MID-CONTINENT PUBLIC LIBRARY

JE
Rowe, Don
The sandbox

MID-CONTINENT PUBLIC LIBRARY
Lee's Summit Branch
150 NW Oldham Parkway
Lee's Summit, MO 64081 **LS**

Dear Parents, Caregivers, and Educators:

This book presents everyday issues that all children face. On page 22, you'll find some questions to help children further explore these issues, both as they are presented in the story, and also as they might apply in the children's own lives. We hope these questions serve as starting points for developing a deeper understanding and appreciation of this book and the challenging situations it presents.

MID-CONTINENT PUBLIC LIBRARY

3 0000 12491435 3

MID-CONTINENT PUBLIC LIBRARY
Lee's Summit Branch
150 NW Oldham Parkway
Lee's Summit, MO 64081 **LS**

First American edition published in 2005 by
Picture Window Books
5115 Excelsior Boulevard
Suite 232
Minneapolis, MN 55416
877-845-8392
www.picturewindowbooks.com

First published in 2001 by
A & C Black (Publishers) Ltd
37 Soho Square
London WID 3QZ

Text copyright © Citizenship Foundation 2001
Illustrations copyright © Tim Archbold 2001

The rights of Don Rowe and Tim Archbold to be identified
as author and illustrator of this work have been asserted by
them in accordance with the Copyrights, Designs and Patents
Act 1988.

All rights reserved. No part of this publication may be reproduced
in any form or by any means—graphic, electronic or mechanical,
including photocopying, recording, taping or information storage and
retrieval systems—without the prior permission in writing of
the publishers.

Published in conjunction with the Citizenship Foundation.
Sponsored by British Telecom.

Printed in the United States of America.

Library of Congress Cataloging-in-Publication Data
Rowe, Don.
The sandbox : a book about fairness / by Don Rowe ; illustrated by
Tim Archbold.
p. cm. — (Making good choices)
Summary: When Mrs. Smith asks Tim and Johnny to let Kylie join the
game they are playing, they do not want to include her.
ISBN 1-4048-0665-2 (hardcover)
[1. Sharing—Fiction. 2. Fairness—Fiction. 3. Schools—Fiction.]
I. Archbold, Tim, ill. II. Title. III. Series.
PZ7.R7936San 2004
[E]—dc22   2004007469

The Sandbox

by Don Rowe

illustrated by Tim Archbold

PICTURE WINDOW BOOKS
Minneapolis, Minnesota

This is Johnny Foster.
He goes to school now because he is five.

He is in Mrs. Smith's class.
Mrs. Smith is very nice.

Johnny likes everything at school.

At recess, he plays with his friend Tim.

Johnny and Tim have been friends since preschool.

One day after lunch, Mrs. Smith said
that Johnny and Tim could play in the sandbox
and make up a story.

Johnny and Tim always made up exciting stories
with the cars from the box.
Today, they decided to play hospital.

Johnny's car crashed into a tree.

Tim's ambulance came to the rescue.

It was their best game ever.

Just then, Mrs. Smith came up,
holding Kylie's hand.

Kylie was crying because
no one wanted to play with her.

When Mrs. Smith asked Kylie
who she wanted to play with,
she said, "Johnny."

Kylie lived next door to Johnny,
and they often played together
at home.

"Boys," said Mrs. Smith, "can Kylie play, too?
She'd like to join in your story game."

"She can go next, Mrs. Smith," said Johnny.
"We're in the middle of the story."

"There are no more good cars," said Tim.
"You can't play without a good car.
Our story is about hospitals and ambulances."

"Well then, Kylie could be a doctor at the hospital,
couldn't she?" said Mrs. Smith, smiling.
"There you are, Kylie."

And Mrs. Smith walked away to see
who was making a lot of noise
over by the classroom door.

Kylie dried her eyes and stood
watching the game for a minute.
"What can I be?" she asked.

"Nothing," said Tim. Then he had another thought.
"You can be the person who watches us."

"That's not fair," said Kylie.
"Mrs. Smith said I could play."

Johnny felt bad inside.
At home, he played with Kylie a lot.

But not at school.
Tim was his best friend at school.

Johnny didn't look at Kylie. Instead, he
kept building the hospital in the sand.
He stood up to look at it. It was good.

Kylie was starting to cry again.
"Stop it, Kylie," said Johnny.

"You're horrible!" shouted Kylie suddenly,
and she knocked Johnny's hospital over
with her foot.

"Stop it, Kylie!" Johnny shouted, and he pushed
her away so hard that she nearly fell over.
This made her cry even more.

The whole class stopped to
look at what was happening.

"Johnny and Tim!" said Mrs. Smith in a loud voice.
"I asked you to share your
game with Kylie."

"Well, if you can't share the sandbox, you'll have to let someone else play there. You know the rules. Now go and wash your hands, and sit down at your tables."

Johnny and Tim sat down in a bad mood
and started to draw a picture.
Sometimes, Johnny liked drawing, but not today.
He wanted to play in the sand.

"It's not fair!" he said.

Kylie stood by the sandbox and started to play on her own, but it was no fun.

"It's not fair!" she said.

Mrs. Smith looked at Johnny, Tim, and the whole class.
"Why can't they play nicely just for once?"
she thought.
"My life would be a lot easier."

"It's not fair!"

Something to think about ...

- What is a friend? What do friends do for each other?

- Can anyone be your friend? When is someone not your friend?

- In the story, Johnny has a problem. What is it?

- Do you think it was fair of Mrs. Smith to ask the boys to let Kylie play with them? Why do you think that?

- Was Johnny wrong when he wouldn't let Kylie play with them? Why or why not?

- What do you think about the way Johnny and Tim behaved? What words can we use to describe this?

- What do you think about what Kylie did when she broke up the game? What words can we use to describe this? Think of some other examples of when people act like this.

- What should happen to Kylie for breaking up the game? Would you be strict with Kylie or not, if you were the teacher? Why?

- Who do you feel most sorry for in the story: Kylie, Johnny, Tim, or Mrs. Smith?

- Why do you think all the people in the story say "It's not fair?" Who do you agree with most? Why is that?

Glossary

ambulance—a vehicle that takes sick or injured people to the hospital

exciting—thrilling or highly interesting

mood—the way that you are feeling

rescue—to save, or to get something or someone out of danger

To Learn More

At the Library
Hall, Kirsten. *Tug-of-War: All About Balance.* New York: Children's Press, 2004.

Kyle, Kathryn. *Fairness.* Chanhassen, Minn.: Child's World, 2003.

Loewen, Nancy. *No Fair! Kids Talk About Fairness.* Minneapolis: Picture Window Books, 2003.

On the Web
FactHound offers a safe, fun way to find Web sites related to this book. All of the sites on FactHound have been researched by our staff. *www.facthound.com*

1. Visit the FactHound home page.
2. Enter a search word related to this book, or type in this special code: 1404806652.
3. Click the FETCH IT button.

Your trusty FactHound will fetch the best Web sites for you!

Look for all of the books in this series:

Joe's Car

The Sandbox

The Scary Movie

William and the Guinea Pig